TWO FAT CAMELS

The Story of Two Rich Men from Luke 18–19

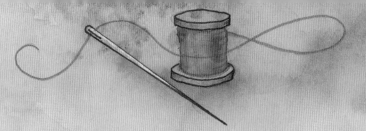

Dedications:

To my mother, Winifred Rose O'Donnell. DSO
To David, Daniel, and Emma, with love. GS

The teachings of Jesus aren't meant for us simply to recite or to use as part of a coloring book. They were designed to provoke and instruct us—to get us thinking and imagining new ways of seeing spiritual reality. This combination of a gifted biblical theologian and a whimsical artist has produced a book that will delight and instruct children, and will leave all of us—child and parent alike—seeing some old stories in a surprising new way. Warmly recommended!

Justin Taylor,
Managing Editor, *The ESV Study Bible*

Two Fat Camels belongs on the reading shelf of young children! For in words put down and pictures well painted, it reminds us of what Jesus said to those hoping to enter into God's kingdom.

David Helm,
Author, *The Big Picture Story Bible*

TWO FAT CAMELS

The Story of Two Rich Men from Luke 18–19

Douglas Sean O'Donnell
Illustrated by Gail Schoonmaker

When Jesus talked about God and His kingdom, sometimes He talked about animals. He talked about fish and dogs and snakes and pigs! Then one day, He talked about a ...

CAMEL

"How hard it is," He said, "for a rich man to enter into the kingdom of God. It is easier for a **CAMEL** to get through the eye of a needle than for a rich man to enter the kingdom of God."

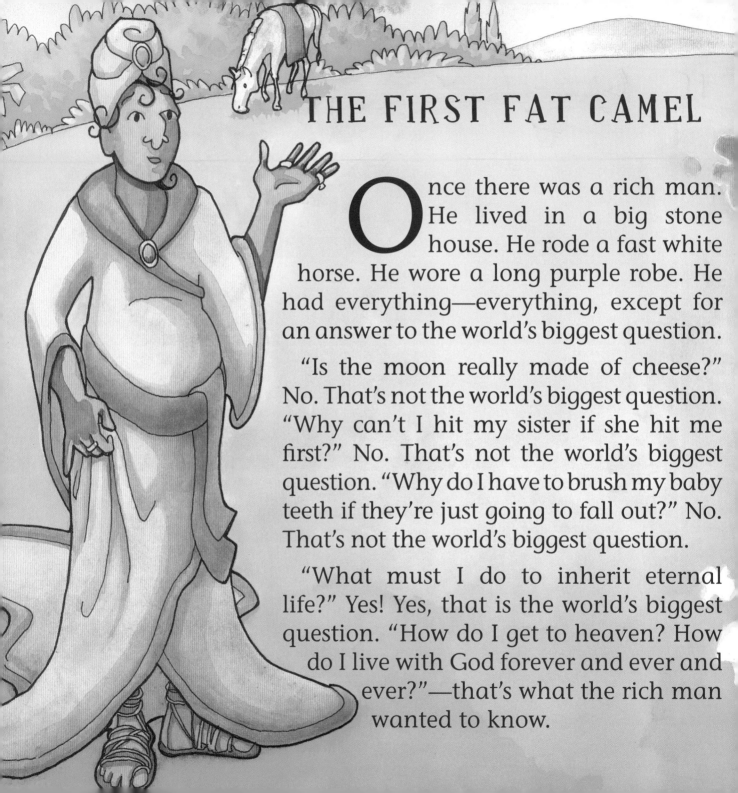

THE FIRST FAT CAMEL

Once there was a rich man. He lived in a big stone house. He rode a fast white horse. He wore a long purple robe. He had everything—everything, except for an answer to the world's biggest question.

"Is the moon really made of cheese?" No. That's not the world's biggest question. "Why can't I hit my sister if she hit me first?" No. That's not the world's biggest question. "Why do I have to brush my baby teeth if they're just going to fall out?" No. That's not the world's biggest question.

"What must I do to inherit eternal life?" Yes! Yes, that is the world's biggest question. "How do I get to heaven? How do I live with God forever and ever and ever?"—that's what the rich man wanted to know.

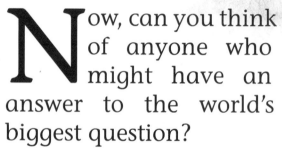

Now, can you think of anyone who might have an answer to the world's biggest question?

Jesus! That's right. And that's just what the rich man thought. So, one day when Jesus came to town the rich man came to Jesus. "Good teacher," he asked, "What must I do to inherit eternal life?"

Jesus looked at him. Jesus loved him. Jesus answered him, "Do you know the Ten Commandments?"

The man smiled. He knew all ten. 1, 2, 3, 4—the first four talk about loving God. 5, 6, 7, 8, 9, 10—the next six talk about loving others. "I know those. I've obeyed those!" the man said. He thought he was so good.

But Jesus knew that only God is good—perfectly good. Jesus also knew that this man had not perfectly obeyed God's commandments, not even the first one. Do you know the first commandment? It is to love God best, more than anything. "There is just one more thing to do," Jesus said. "Go and sell all that you have and give it to the poor. Then, come and follow me."

Jesus was testing this man's heart. Did he really love God more than everything? Was he willing to give up everything to follow Jesus?

The rich man was not expecting this. He scratched his head. "Sell everything? My big stone house? My fast white horse? My long purple robe?"

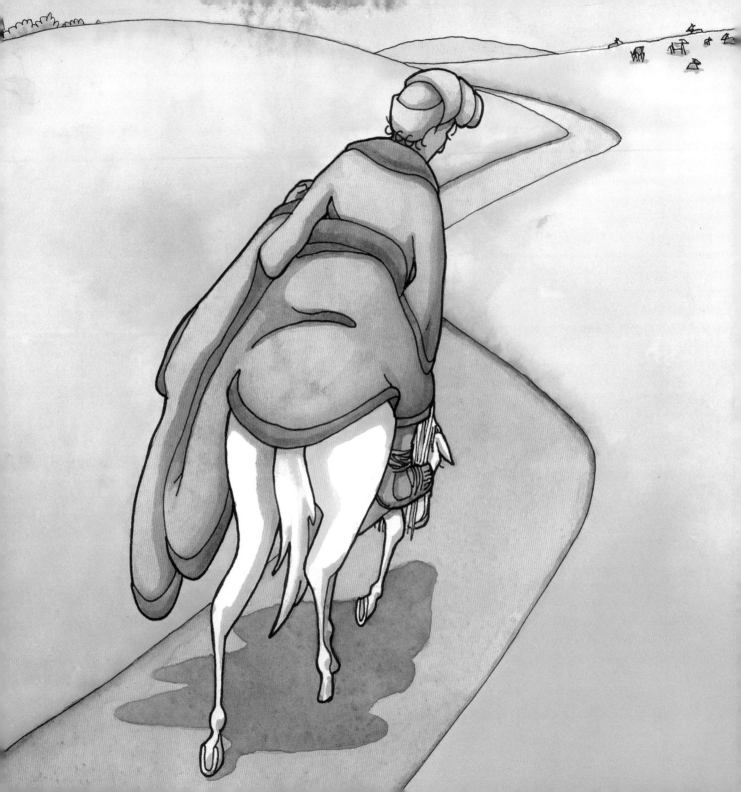

A tear welled up in his eye. It hit the ground as he hung his head. "No, I can't. I just can't." He pulled up his long robe. He mounted his horse. He rode away, back to his house. He loved these things more than God.

Now it was when the rich man turned away from Jesus that Jesus turned to His followers. They were men and women who had given away everything to follow Him. And that's when He said what He said about the **CAMEL**. Remember? He said, "How hard it is for a rich man to enter into the kingdom of God. It is easier for a **CAMEL** to get through the eye of a needle than for a rich man to enter the kingdom of God."

Does this mean that being rich is bad? No! It is loving money more than God that is bad. Why? Because when we have lots of money and lots of stuff, it's hard to love Jesus most of all.

LOOKING THROUGH THE NEEDLE

Have you ever seen a **CAMEL**? It's bigger than a fish. It's bigger than a snake. It's bigger than a dog. It's bigger than a pig. Oink! Oink! It's bigger than 52 big brothers stepping on your toes. Ouch! That would hurt. **CAMELS** are big. But NEEDLES are small. Have you ever seen a needle? Not the kind the doctor uses. Ouch! That would hurt too! I mean the kind used for sewing on buttons. Maybe your grandmother has one.

A needle is small; and the eye of a needle even smaller. The eye of the needle is that little, itty bitty hole your grandmother pushes the thread through. Do you have a bellybutton? Take your finger and put it there. Don't laugh. This is important. An eye of a needle is smaller than that.

So, what do you think? Do you think a BIG **CAMEL** can fit through a small needle? There's no way. A BIG **CAMEL**—a small needle—it's impossible. Or is it?

Jesus once said, "With man it is impossible, but with God all things are possible." Let's see what God can do!

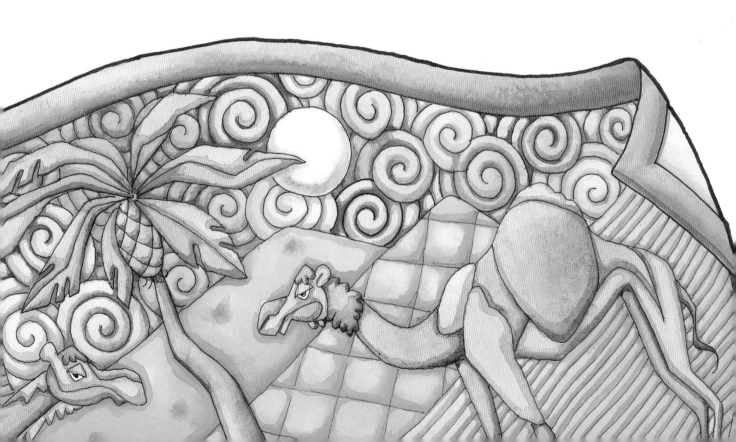

THE SECOND FAT CAMEL

Once there was a rich man, another rich man. Our second fat camel! The Bible tells us his name was Zacchaeus. He was very, very rich, but also very, very small.

Think of the tallest man you know—maybe your dad or uncle. Zacchaeus was half his size.

That's what he looked like on the outside. But on the inside he was as big as a 2000-pound camel.

I know we shouldn't call people "fat." But that is what he was.

To Jesus, he was like a **FAT CAMEL**.

Fat, not because he ate too many cupcakes or drank too many milkshakes. He was fat because his heart was full of the love of money. Just like that other rich man, he loved money more than people. He loved money more than God. That's what made him so fat.

Well, one day this fat **CAMEL** had enough!!! Zacchaeus wanted to be small on the inside, much smaller than he was. He wanted to be small enough to enter the kingdom of God. So here's what he did. He became like a little child, the smallest little boy in the whole wide world. It all started on the day that Jesus arrived.

"Jesus is coming to town! Jesus is coming to town!" Jesus was coming into Jericho, the town where Zacchaeus lived. Everyone liked Jesus and wanted to see Him, even Zacchaeus, the chief tax collector, the one man in town no one liked. No one liked him because he collected money for the government and always kept some for himself. The big crowd that gathered was so big that little Zacchaeus couldn't see. So, here's what he did.

(It's kind of funny.)

L ike a five-year-old boy running after the ice cream
truck on a hot summer day, he ran ahead of the
crowd. He ran to the foot of a sycamore tree. "Ah!"
said the little man, "I know what I'll do."

He looked up. He climbed up. He waited. Zacchaeus wasn't hiding in the tree. He was seeking! The Bible tells us—he was seeking Jesus. "Who is this Jesus?" he wondered as he waited.

The noise of the crowd came closer. No one noticed the little man in the tree. No one, but Jesus! Jesus stopped. He looked. He spoke. "Zacchaeus," He said. Jesus knew his name. "Hurry up!" He said. "Come down," He said. "Today I must stay at your house!"

Zacchaeus didn't think twice. He climbed down the tree. The crowd backed up as he walked closer to Jesus. No one liked Zacchaeus. They mumbled mean words under their breath—

"Does Jesus know what a bad man he is? He loves money so much that he steals it from us. What a fat **CAMEL**. Stay away from him!"

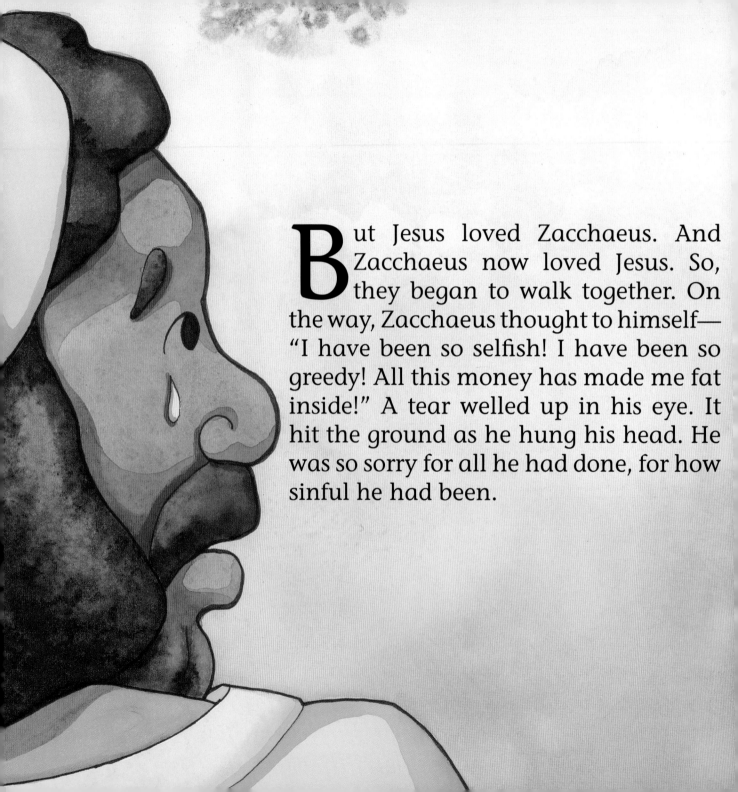

But Jesus loved Zacchaeus. And Zacchaeus now loved Jesus. So, they began to walk together. On the way, Zacchaeus thought to himself— "I have been so selfish! I have been so greedy! All this money has made me fat inside!" A tear welled up in his eye. It hit the ground as he hung his head. He was so sorry for all he had done, for how sinful he had been.

Zacchaeus wiped his eyes. "I know what I'll do," he said to himself. "I'll show I'm sorry! I'll show how I now love God and people more than money. I will give my money to those in need and to everyone I have robbed. I am willing to give everything away to follow Jesus!"

That's what he thought. And that's just what he did.

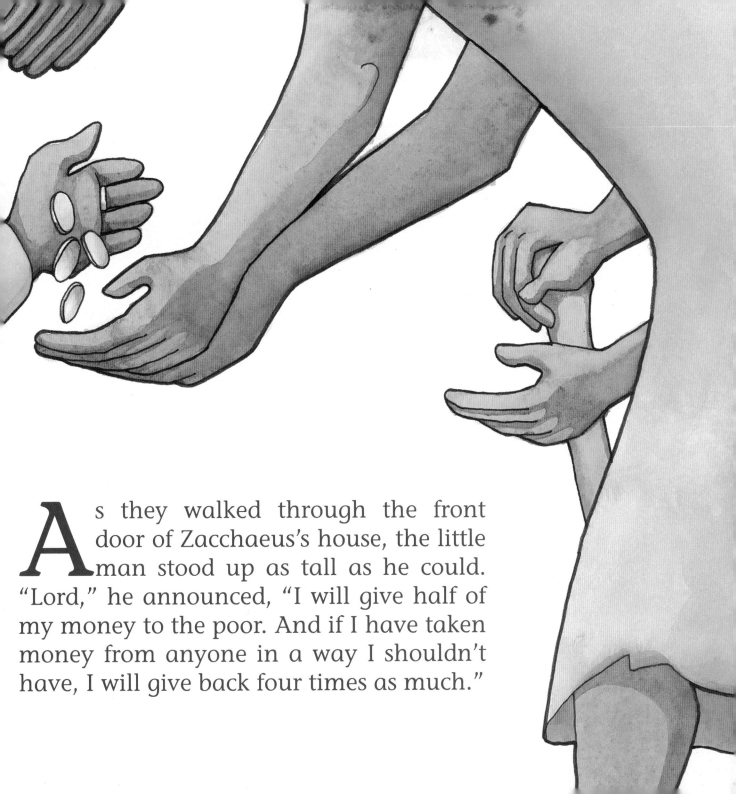

As they walked through the front door of Zacchaeus's house, the little man stood up as tall as he could. "Lord," he announced, "I will give half of my money to the poor. And if I have taken money from anyone in a way I shouldn't have, I will give back four times as much."

He sat down. Happy. So happy. Do you remember when the other rich man walked away? He was so sad. So sad. He didn't want to follow Jesus. He didn't want to give away his money. But do you see what is so different with Zacchaeus?

Jesus didn't even have to tell him to give. No. His heart was changed. He trusted in Jesus completely. He loved God best of all. And Jesus knew it. This is why Jesus said to Zacchaeus, "Salvation has come to this house."

Do you see what happened? Zacchaeus—once a rich man, a **FAT CAMEL**—made it into heaven, through the eye of the needle! He made it through because he believed that trusting in Jesus (not his money!) was the only way into the kingdom, the only way to live with God forever and ever.

Amazing? Yes. Impossible? No.

Luke 18:18-30

And a ruler asked him, "Good Teacher, what must I do to inherit eternal life?" And Jesus said to him, "Why do you call me good? No one is good except God alone. You know the commandments: 'Do not commit adultery, Do not murder, Do not steal, Do not bear false witness, Honor your father and mother.' And he said, "All these I have kept from my youth." When Jesus heard this, he said to him, "One thing you still lack. Sell all that you have and distribute to the poor, and you will have treasure in heaven; and come, follow me." But when he heard these things, he became very sad, for he was extremely rich.

Jesus, seeing that he had become sad, said, "How difficult it is for those who have wealth to enter the kingdom of God! For it is easier for a camel to go through the eye of a needle than for a rich person to enter the kingdom of God." Those who heard it said, "Then who can be saved?" But he said, "What is impossible with man is possible with God." And Peter said, "See, we have left our homes and followed you." And he said to them, "Truly, I say to you, there is no one who has left house or wife or brothers or parents or children, for the sake of the kingdom of God, who will not receive many times more in this time, and in the age to come eternal life."

Luke 19:1-10

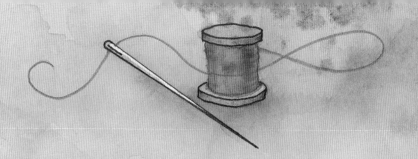

He (Jesus) entered Jericho and was passing through. And behold, there was a man named Zacchaeus. He was a chief tax collector and was rich. And he was seeking to see who Jesus was, but on account of the crowd he could not, because he was small in stature. So he ran on ahead and climbed up into a sycamore tree to see him, for he was about to pass that way. And when Jesus came to the place, he looked up and said to him, "Zacchaeus, hurry and come down, for I must stay at your house today."

So he hurried and came down and received him joyfully. And when they saw it, they all grumbled, "He has gone in to be the guest of a man who is a sinner." And Zacchaeus stood and said to the Lord, "Behold, Lord, the half of my goods I give to the poor. And if I have defrauded anyone of anything, I restore it fourfold." And Jesus said to him, "Today salvation has come to this house, since he also is a son of Abraham. For the Son of Man came to seek and to save the lost."

Christian Focus Publications publishes books for adults and children under its four main imprints:
Christian Focus, CF4K, Mentor and Christian Heritage. Our books reflect our conviction that God's Word is reliable
and Jesus is the way to know him, and live for ever with him.
Our children's publication list includes a Sunday School curriculum that covers pre-school to early teens, and puzzle
and activity books. We also publish personal and family devotional titles, biographies and inspirational stories that
children will love. If you are looking for quality Bible teaching for children then we have an excellent range of Bible
stories and age-specific theological books. From pre-school board books to teenage apologetics, we have it covered!

Find us at our web page: www.christianfocus.com

10 9 8 7 6 5 4 3 2 1

Copyright © 2015 Douglas Sean O'Donnell

ISBN: 978-1-78191-562-2

Published by Christian Focus Publications, Geanies House, Fearn, Tain, Ross-shire,
IV20 1TW, Scotland, U.K.

Cover design: Daniel van Straaten

Illustrations by Gail Schoonmaker

Printed in China